What Is Your
Baby
Really Thinking?

WHAT IS YOUR BABY REALLY THINKING?

Copyright © Summersdale Publishers Ltd, 2020

Text by Anna Martin

Illustrations by Dannyboy

An Hachette UK Company
www.hachette.co.uk

Summersdale Publishers Ltd
Part of Octopus Publishing Group Limited
Carmelite House
50 Victoria Embankment
LONDON
EC4Y 0DZ
UK

www.summersdale.com

Printed and bound in the Czech Republic

ISBN: 978-1-78783-265-7

Substantial discounts on bulk quantities of Summersdale books are available to corporations, professional associations and other organizations. For details contact general enquiries: telephone: +44 (0) 1243 771107 or email: enquiries@summersdale.com.

What Is Your
Baby
Really Thinking?

Dannyboy
and Sam Hart

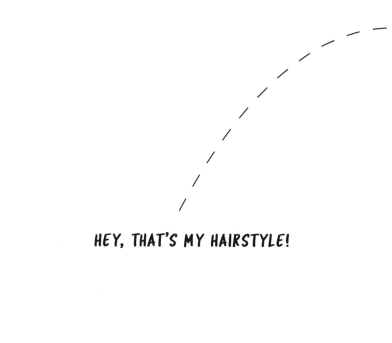

HEY, THAT'S MY HAIRSTYLE!

IT DOESN'T MATTER HOW
HIGH I JUMP, I CAN'T SEEM TO
ESCAPE THIS FUNKY SMELL.

I DON'T WANT TO BE IN THE BATH...
I'LL GET A SHRIVELLED FACE
LIKE GRANDMA.

NOT JOAN AGAIN, GOING ON
ABOUT HER WEAK PELVIC FLOOR.

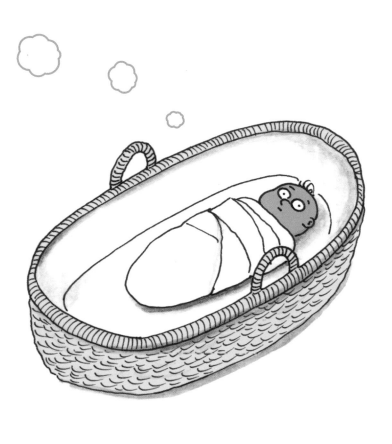

CALL OFF THE TRIP TO THE SALON;
I'VE JUST POOPED MY PANTS.

DO YOU REALIZE THERE ARE 84 TYPES OF
BACTERIA SWIMMING IN THIS BALL PIT?

I'M JUST A SWEATER TO YOU, AREN'T I?
WAIT TILL MUM HEARS ABOUT THIS.

IF I GET IT IN THE EYE,
THAT'S 50 POINTS.

YOU'RE FIRED!

WHY DOESN'T MILK COME
OUT OF THIS TOO?

IT'S MY HAIRY BROTHER!
WHEN DO I GET MY TAIL?

LET ME TELL YOU SOMETHING:
IT'S GOING TO BE AT LEAST
ANOTHER 18 YEARS BEFORE
YOU GET TO SLEEP IN...

LOVE THE CRINKLY WRINKLY STUFF!

SO IF I CRY, I GET MILK?

IT'S PLANK TIME — AND MAKE SURE YOU
TELL ME HOW MANY LIKES I GET ON
SOCIAL MEDIA WHEN YOU POST IT.

THAT'LL TEACH YOU NOT
TO PICK UP MY TOYS AFTER ME!

WHY DOES SHE KEEP GRABBING MY
TOES AND SINGING ABOUT FISH?

THE FIRST THING I'M GOING TO DO WHEN I'VE
LEARNED TO TALK IS TELL YOU TO "ZIP IT".

WE NEED TO HAVE A SERIOUS TALK
ABOUT YOUR COOKING SKILLS.

NEED HUGS! NEED MILK!
I'VE POOOOOOOOPED!

NOT IMPRESSED WITH THE
WI-FI ROUND HERE.

JUST MARKING MY TERRITORY.

I'LL JUST PUT THIS IN HERE
TO KEEP IT SAFE FOR LATER.

NOW WE CAN SPEND MORE
TIME IN THE PARK!

WHO TOOK MY TOES?

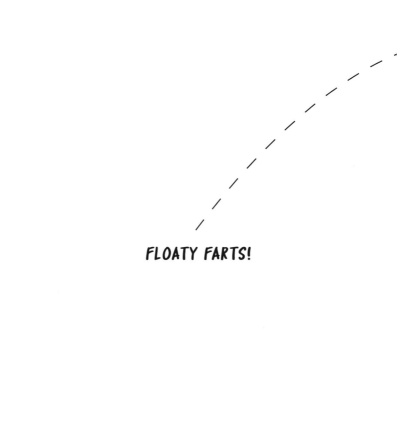

FLOATY FARTS!

I DON'T KNOW WHO THE CUTEST LITTLE BUBBSY, WUBBSY IS. HURRY UP AND TELL ME, WON'T YOU?

SO WHAT DO YOU MAKE OF THE LATEST
EPISODE OF *THE BACHELOR?*

DON'T TAKE MY NOSE!
HE'S TAKING MY NOSE!
CALL THE POLICE!

THIS STORY DOESN'T TASTE GOOD.
READ ME ANOTHER ONE!

MY FAVOURITE TOY –
A POOP FISH!

ELEPHANT!

VACUUM CLEANER!

DO ALL TREES COME INSIDE
WHEN THEY GET COLD?

I DON'T WANT TO
EAT AN AEROPLANE.

NAILED IT.

If you're interested in finding out more about our books,
find us on Facebook at **Summersdale Publishers**
and follow us on Twitter at **@Summersdale**.

www.summersdale.com